ISBN 978-0-259-59315-7
PIBN 10823877

This book is a reproduction of an important historical work. Forgotten Books uses
state-of-the-art technology to digitally reconstruct the work, preserving the original format
whilst repairing imperfections present in the aged copy. In rare cases, an imperfection in
the original, such as a blemish or missing page, may be replicated in our edition. We do,
however, repair the vast majority of imperfections successfully; any imperfections that
remain are intentionally left to preserve the state of such historical works.

# 1 MONTH OF
# FREE
# READING

## at
## www.ForgottenBooks.com

By purchasing this book you are eligible for one month membership to ForgottenBooks.com, giving you unlimited access to our entire collection of over 1,000,000 titles via our web site and mobile apps.

To claim your free month visit:
www.forgottenbooks.com/free823877

English
Français
Deutsche
Italiano
Español
Português

# www.forgottenbooks.com

**Mythology** Photography **Fiction**
Fishing Christianity **Art** Cooking
Essays Buddhism Freemasonry
Medicine **Biology** Music **Ancient**
**Egypt** Evolution Carpentry Physics
Dance Geology **Mathematics** Fitness
Shakespeare **Folklore** Yoga Marketing
**Confidence** Immortality Biographies
Poetry **Psychology** Witchcraft
Electronics Chemistry History **Law**
Accounting **Philosophy** Anthropology
Alchemy Drama Quantum Mechanics
Atheism Sexual Health **Ancient History**
**Entrepreneurship** Languages Sport
Paleontology Needlework Islam
**Metaphysics** Investment Archaeology
Parenting Statistics Criminology
**Motivational**

# SPIRITUAL FACTS

CONSISTING OF SELECTIONS FROM

## SWEDENBORG'S

## HEAVEN

AND THE

## WORLD OF SPIRITS

AND

## HELL

---

SWEDENBORG PRINTING BUREAU
16 ARLINGTON STREET
BOSTON

# SPIRITUAL FACTS.

Consisting of Selections from Swedenborg's "Heaven and Hell, from Things Heard and Seen." Originally published in 1758.

---

## SWEDENBORG'S MISSION.

The man of the Church at this day knows scarce anything of heaven and hell, or of his own life after death, although these things are all described in the Word. Indeed, many who are born within the Church even deny them, saying in their heart, Who has come from that world and told us? Lest therefore such denial, prevailing especially with those who have much worldly wisdom, should also infect and corrupt the simple in heart and the simple in faith, it has been given me to be in company with angels and to talk with them as man with man, and also to see what is in the heavens and what is in the hells, and this for thirteen years. Therefore I can now describe these things from what I have heard and seen, in the hope that thus ignorance may be enlightened and unbelief dispelled. That at this day such immediate revelation exists, is because this is what is meant by the coming of the Lord.

## WHAT THE WORLD OF SPIRITS IS.

The world of spirits is not heaven, nor is it hell, but it is the middle place or state between the two; for it is the place into which man first comes after death, and from which after his appointed time he is, according to his life in the world, either elevated into heaven or cast into hell.

Almost every man at this day is in such a state that he knows truths, and from

2

knowledge and also from understanding thinks them, and either does much of them or little of them, or does nothing of them, or acts contrary to them from the love ot evil and consequent faith of what is false. Therefore in order that he may have either heaven or hell, he is after death first brought into the world of spirits, and there a conjunction of good and truth is effected with those who are to be elevated into heaven, and a conjunction of evil and falsity with those who are to be cast into hell.

## NO FIXED TERM FOR CONTINUANCE THERE.

In the world of spirits there are vast numbers, because the first meeting of all is there, and all are there explored and prepared. There is no fixed term for their continuance there; some only enter that world and are presently either taken away into heaven or cast down into hell; some remain there only for weeks, some for several years, but not more than thirty.

## FRIENDS MEET THERE.

Men after death as soon as they come into the world of spirits, are clearly distinguished by the Lord; the evil are at once attached to the infernal society in which they were in the world as to their ruling love; and the good are at once attached to the heavenly society in which they were in the world as to love, charity, and faith. But though they are thus divided, still they who have been friends and acquaintances in the life of the body, all meet and converse together, when they desire it, especially wives and husbands and brothers and sisters.

But when they have come from the world of spirits into heaven, or into hell, they then see each other no more, nor know each other, unless they are of a similar disposition, from similar love.

## MAN IS A SPIRIT AS TO HIS INTERIORS.

The body does not think, because it is material, but the soul thinks, because it is spiritual. The soul of man — upon the immortality of which many have written — is his spirit, for this is immortal in all particulars. This also is what thinks in the body, for it is spiritual, and what is spiritual receives what is spiritual and lives spiritually, which is to think and to will. All the rational life, therefore, which appears in the body is of the soul, and nothing of the body. When the body is separated from its spirit, which is called dying, the man remains still a man, and lives.

## DIFFERENCE BETWEEN MEN AND BEASTS.

The spiritual of beasts is not such as the spiritual of man is; for man has, and beasts have not, an inmost, into which the Divine flows and elevates to Itself, and by it conjoins to Itself.

## MEN IN SOCIETY WITH SPIRITS.

Every man, even while he lives in the body, is as to his spirit in society with spirits, though he does not know it; a good man through them in an angelic society, and an evil man in an infernal society; and into the same society he comes after death.

## MAN'S RESUSCITATION FROM THE DEAD.

When the body is no longer able to discharge its functions in the natural world then man is said to die. This takes place when the breathing of the lungs and beating of the heart cease; yet the man does not die, but is only separated from the bodily part which he had for use in the world, and the man himself lives. From this it is plain that man when he dies, he only passes from one world into another. Hence it is that death, in the Word, in its internal

4

sense signifies resurrection and continuation of life.

## RAISED BY THE LORD ALONE.

The spirit of man, after the separation. remains a little while in the body, but not longer than till the total cessation of the heart's action, which takes place with variety according to the condition of disease from which man dies. As soon as this motion ceases, the man is raised again: but this is done by the Lord alone.

## HOW MAN IS RAISED AGAIN.

How man is raised again has not only been told me, but also shown by living experience. The actual experience was given me in order that I might fully know how it is.

I was brought into a state of insensibility as to the bodily senses, thus almost into the state of the dying; yet the interior life with thought remaining entire, so that I perceived and retained in memory the things which occurred, and which occur to those who are raised from the dead. I perceived that the respiration of the body was almost taken away, the interior respiration of the spirit remaining, connected with a slight and tacit respiration of the body. Then there was first given communication as to the pulse of the heart with the celestial kingdom, Angels from it were also seen, some at a distance, and two near the head, at which they were seated. I was in this state for some hours. Then the spirits who were around me withdrew. thinking that I was dead. The angels who were seated at the head were silent. only communicating their thoughts with mine, and when these are received the angels know that the spirit is in such a state that it can be drawn forth from the body. The communication of their thoughts was made by looking into my face.

## CELESTIAL ANGELS WITH THOSE WHO ARE RAISED.

When the celestial angels are with one who is raised again, they do not leave him, because they love every one; but when his spirit is such that he can not be longer in company with celestial angels, he desires to depart from them; and when this is the case, angels come from the Lord's spiritual kingdom, by whom is given to him the use of light; for before he saw nothing, but only thought.

## SPIRITUAL ANGELS FOLLOW THE CELESTIAL ANGELS.

The spiritual angels, after the use of light has been given, perform for the new spirit all the services which he can ever desire in that state, and instruct him in regard to the things of another life, but only so far as he can comprehend. If however he is not such as to be willing to be instructed, the spirit then desires to depart from the company of the angels. The angels do not indeed leave him, but he separates himself from them. When the spirit thus separates himself, he is received by good spirits, and when he is in their company also, all kind services are performed for him; but if his life in the world had been such that he could not be in the company of the good, then he wishes to remove also from them; and this even until he associates himself with such as agree altogether with his life in the world, with whom he finds his own life; and then, what is wonderful, he leads a similar life to what he led in the world. But this beginning of man's life after death continues only for a few days.

## MAN AFTER DEATH IN HUMAN FORM

That the spirit of man after being loosed from the body is a man, and in a similar form, has been proved to me by the daily

6

experience of many years; for I have seen and heard them a thousand times; for I have spoken with them on this very point, that men in the world do not believe them to be men, and that those who do believe, are thought simple by the learned.

Almost all who come from the world wonder very much that they are alive. and that they are men equally as before, that they see, hear, and speak, and that their body has the sense of touch as before and there is no difference at all.

## MAN AFTER DEATH IN ALL HIS FACULTIES.

Man when he enters the spiritual world. or the life after death, is in a body as in the world; to appearance there is no difference, since he does not perceive nor see any distinction. But his body is then spiritual, and thus separated or purified from what is earthly, and when what is spiritual touches and sees what is spiritual, it is just as when what is natural touches and sees what is natural: hence a man, when he has become a spirit, does not know but that he is in his body in which he was in the world, and thus does not know that he has died. A man spirit also enjoys every sense, both outer and inner, which he enjoyed in the world; he sees as before, he hears and speaks as before, he also smells and tastes, and when he is touched, he feels the touch as before: he also longs, desires, craves, thinks, reflects, is affected. loves, wills, as before; and he who is delighted with studies, reads and writes as before. In a word. when a man passes from one life into the other, or from one world into the other, it is as if he passed from one place into another; and he carries with him all things which he possessed in himself as a man, so that it cannot be said that the man after death, which is only the death of the earthly body, has lost anything of himself. He also carries with him the natural memory, for he retains all things that he has in the world heard, seen, read, learned and thought, from earliest infancy even to the end of life.

## THE BOOK OF LIFE.

Man has an outer and inner memory, an outer memory of his natural man, and an inner, of his spiritual man; and every thing which man has thought, willed, spoken, done, or even heard and seen, is inscribed on his inner or spiritual memory; and what is there is never erased, since it is inscribed at the same time on the spirit itself and on the members of its body; and thus the spirit is formed according to the thoughts and deeds of its will.

From these things it may be evident what is meant by the book of man's life, spoken of in the Word.

## HOW THE RATIONAL FACULTY MAY BE CULTIVATED.

The genuine rational faculty consists of truths, and not of falsities. Truths are of threefold order, civil, moral, and spiritual. Civil truths relate to the things of judgment and government in kingdoms, in general to what is just and equitable in them. Moral truths relate to the things of every man's life in regard to companionships and social relations, in general to what is sincere and right, and in particular to virtues of every kind. But spiritual truths relate to the things of heaven and of the church, in general to the good of love and the truth of faith. There are three degrees of life with every man. The rational faculty is opened to the first degree by civil truths, to the second degree by moral truths, and to the third degree by spiritual truths. But it is to be known that the rational faculty from these truths is not formed and opened by man's knowing them, but by his living according to them.

8

# THE FIRST STATE OF MAN AFTER DEATH.

There are three states which man passes through after death, before he comes either into heaven or into hell; the first state is that of his exteriors, the second is that of his interiors, and the third is that of his preparation. Man passes through these states in the world of spirits. There are some however who do not pass through these states, but immediately after death are either taken up into heaven or cast into hell. But all these are few in comparison with those who are kept in the world of spirits and there according to Divine order undergo preparation for heaven, or for hell.

The first state of man after death is similar to his state in the world, because he is then in like manner in his exteriors; he has also a similar face, similar speech, and a similar disposition, thus a similar moral and civil life. And so he does not know but he is still in the world, unless he pays attention to the things that he meets and to what was said to him by the angels, when he was raised up, that he is now a spirit. Thus one life is continued into the other, and death is only the passage. Hence all when they first come into the other life are recognized by their friends, their relatives, and those known to them in any way; and they talk together and afterward associate, according to their friendship in the world. I have frequently heard that those who have come from the world rejoiced at seeing their friends again, and that their friends on their part rejoiced that they had come. Very commonly a husband and wife come together and congratulate each other. And they remain together, but this for a longer or a shorter time, according to their delight in living together in the world. If true marriage love, which is the conjunction of minds from heavenly love, has not united them, after

9

remaining together some time they are separated. And if the minds of the parties were in disagreement and were inwardly averse to each other, they burst forth into open enmity and sometimes into combat; notwithstanding which they are not separated until they enter the second state.

Spirits recently from the world after wondering that they are in a body and in every sense which they had in the world, and that they see similar objects, become eager to know what heaven is, what hell is, and where they are. They are then instructed by friends in regard to the state of eternal life, and are led about to various places and into various companies, and some times into cities — also into gardens and paradises — in general to magnificent things, such as delight the outward senses they then have. Then by turns they are brought into their thoughts which they had in the life of the body, in regard to the state of their soul after death, and heaven and hell.

All the spirits who arrive from the world are indeed attached to some society in heaven, or to some society in hell, but only as to their interiors.

This first state of man after death continues with some for days, with some for months, and with some for a year; but seldom with any one beyond a year.

## SECOND STATE OF MAN AFTER DEATH.

When the first state is passed through, the man-spirit is let into the state of his interiors, in which he had been in the world when left to himself to think freely and without restraint. Into this state he glides without being aware of it. When the man-spirit is in this state, he is in himself and in his very life.

He who was interiorly in good in the world, then acts rationally and wisely, indeed, more wisely than in the world, because he is released from connection with the body, and thus from terrestrial things. But he who was in evil in the world, then acts foolishly and insanely, even more insanely than in the world, because he is in freedom and under no restraint.

When spirits are in this second state, they appear just such as they had been in themselves in the world, and what they had done and spoken in concealment is made manifest; for then, as no outward considerations restrain them, they speak and endeavor to act openly in the same way as they had before done in secret, not being afraid for their reputation as in the world.

## EVIL SPIRITS IN THE SECOND STATE.

Evil spirits, when they are in this second state, inasmuch as they rush into evils of every kind, are wont to be frequently and grievously punished. No one in the other world suffers punishment on account of the evils which he had done in this world, but on account of the evils which he then does.

Every one comes to his own society in which his spirit has been in the world; for every man as to his spirit is conjoined to some society, either infernal or heavenly — a wicked man to an infernal society, a good man to a heavenly society — to which he returns after death. The spirit is brought to that society by successive steps and at length enters it.

The separation of evil spirits from good spirits is effected in this second state; for in the first state they are together.

## THIRD STATE AFTER DEATH, WHICH IS THAT OF INSTRUCTION FOR HEAVEN.

The third state of man after death is a state of instruction. This state is for those who come into heaven and become angels, but not for those who come into hell; since these cannot be instructed and their second state is therefore also their third.

Instructions are given by angels of many societies. The good spirits who are to be instructed are brought thither by the Lord when they have passed through their second state in the world of spirits, but still not all; for those who have been instructed in the world have also been prepared there by the Lord for heaven, and are taken up into heaven by another way — some immediately after death, some after a short stay with good spirits, where the grosser things of their thoughts and affections, which they contracted from honors and riches in the world, are removed, and thus they are purified.

But all are not instructed alike, nor by like societies of heaven. They who from infancy have been educated in heaven, are instructed by angels of the interior heavens.

They who have died adult are mostly instructed by angels of the lowest heaven. because these angels are better suited to them than the angels of the interior heavens.

When spirits have been prepared for heaven they are then clothed with angelic garments, and thus they are brought to the way which tends upward to heaven. and are delivered to angel guards there. and are then received by other angels and introduced into societies, and into many blessed things. Afterward every one is led by the Lord into his own society.

## MOHAMMEDANS AND PAGAN SPIRITS.

The Mohammedans are instructed by angels who had been in the world in the same religion, and had been converted to Christianity. The heathen likewise are instructed by their respective angels. The Mohammedans and the heathen, are instructed from doctrines adapted to their apprehension, which differ from heavenly doctrine only in this, that spiritual life is taught by moral life in agreement with the good dogmas of their religion.

## NO ONE COMES INTO HEAVEN FROM IMMEDIATE MERCY.

Most of those who come from the Christian word into the other life bring with them this faith, that they are to be saved by immediate mercy, for they implore that mercy. They are therefore told that heaven is not denied by the Lord to any one, and that they may be let in and ever stay there, if they desire it. They who desire this have also been admitted, but when they were at the first threshold, they were seized with such anguish of heart from the approach of heavenly heat, that they perceived in themselves infernal torment instead of heavenly joy, and being struck with dismay they cast themselves down headlong. Thus they were instructed by living experience that heaven cannot be given to any one from immediate mercy.

## NOT DIFFICULT TO LIVE THE LIFE THAT LEADS TO HEAVEN.

Some believe that to live the life that leads to heaven, is difficult, because they have been told that man must renounce the world, divest himself of the lusts called lusts of the body and the flesh, and live spiritually. And by this they understand that they must reject worldly things, which consist chiefly in riches and honors; that they must walk continually in pious meditation about God, about salvation, and about eternal life; and that they must pass their life in prayers, and in reading the Word and pious books. This they suppose to be renouncing the world, and living in the spirit and not in the flesh. But by much experience and from conversation with angels, I have learned that this is not so at all, and indeed that they who renounce the world and live in the spirit in this manner, procure to themselves a sorrowful life, which is not receptive of heavenly joy. But in order that man may receive the life of heaven, he must needs live in the world and engage in its business and employments, and then by moral and civil life receive spiritual life.

It is only necessary for a man to think, when anything presents itself to him which he knows to be insincere and unjust and to which he is inclined, that it ought not to be done because it is contrary to the Divine precepts. If a man accustoms himself so to think, and from so accustoming himself acquires a habit, he then by degrees is conjoined to heaven.

## THE LORD IS THE GOD OF HEAVEN.

First it is to be known who the God of heaven is, since on this all else depends. In the universal heaven none other is acknowledged as the God of heaven than the Lord alone. They say there, as He Himself taught, that He is one with the Father; that the Father is in Him, and He in the Father; that he who sees Him sees the Father; and that all the Holy proceeds from Him.

They within the Church who have denied the Lord and acknowledged only the Father, and have confirmed themselves in such belief, are out of heaven. They who have denied the Divine of the Lord and have acknowledged only His human nature, as the Socinians, are likewise out of heaven. Those who say that they believe in an invisible Divine, which they call the Being [Ens] of the universe, from which all things had their existence, and reject belief in regard to the Lord, are shown by experience that they believe in no God; because the invisible Divine is to them something like nature in her first principles. These are sent away among those who are called Naturalists.

# THE DIVINE OF THE LORD MAKES HEAVEN.

The angels taken together are called heaven, because they constitute heaven; but yet it is the Divine proceeding from the Lord, which flows in with angels and is received by them, that makes heaven. Spirits who while they lived in the world have confirmed themselves in the belief that the good they do and the truth they believe are from themselves, or appropriated to them as their own — in which belief are all who place merit in good deeds and claim to themselves righteousness — are not received into heaven.

## THERE ARE THREE HEAVENS.

There are three heavens, and these wholly distinct from one another, the inmost or third, the middle or second, and the lowest or first.

The interiors of man, which are of his mind and disposition, are also in like order. He has an inmost, a middle and an outmost part.

The Divine which flows in from the Lord and is received in the third or inmost heaven, is called celestial; and hence, the angels there are called celestial angels. The Divine which flows in from the Lord and is received in the second or middle heaven, is called spiritual; and hence the angels there are called spiritual angels. But the Divine which flows in from the Lord and is received in the lowest or first heaven, is called natural. As, however, the natural of that heaven is not like the natural of the world, but has in itself what is spiritual and celestial, that heaven is called spiritual and celestial natural, and hence the angels there are called spiritual and celestial natural.

Because of this distinction, an angel of one heaven cannot enter among angels of another heaven, that is, no one can ascend from a lower heaven, and no one can descend from a higher heaven.

## CONTINUOUS AND DISCREET DEGREES.

There are degrees of two kinds, degrees that are continuous and degrees that are not continuous. Continuous degrees are as the degrees of the waning of light from flame to its obscurity, or as the degrees of the fading of sight from what is in light to what is in shade, or as the degrees of purity of the atmosphere from its highest to its lowest level. These degrees are determined by the distance: whereas degrees not continuous but discrete, are distinguished as what is prior and what is posterior, as cause and effect, and as what produces and what is produced. He who does not gain a perception of these degrees. can in no way learn the distinctions of the heavens, and of man's interior and exterior faculties; nor the distinction between the spiritual and the natural world, and that between the spirit of man and his body.

With every angel, and also with every man, there is an inmost or supreme degree, into which the Lord's Divine first flows. This inmost or supreme degree may be called the Lord's entrance to the angel and to the man, and His veriest dwelling-place with them.

## THE HEAVENS CONSIST OF INNUMERABLE SOCIETIES.

The angels of one heaven are not all together in one place, but are distinguished into societies larger and smaller. according to the differences of the good of love and faith in which they are. Those who are in similar good form one society.

All who are in similar good also know one another. just as men in the world do their kinsmen. their near relations. and their friends. though they have never before seen them; for the reason that in the other life there are no other kinships, relationships and friendships than such as are spiritual.

All the societies of heaven communicate with one another, not by open intercourse — for few go out of their own society into another, since to go out of their society is like going out from themselves, or from their own life, and to pass into another not so well suited to them — but all communicate by extension of the sphere which goes forth from every one's life.

## THE ENTIRE HEAVEN REPRESENTS ONE MAN.

That heaven as one whole represents one man, is an arcanum not yet known in the world, but very well known in the heavens. To know this fact, is the chief thing in the intelligence of the angels in heaven.

The angels do not, indeed, see heaven as a whole in the form of man, since the whole heaven does not fall into the view of any angel; but at times they see distant societies, consisting of many thousands of angels, as a one in such a form; and from a society, as a part, they conclude as to the whole, which is heaven.

## EACH ANGEL IN PERFECT HUMAN FORM.

That angels are human forms, or men, has been seen by me a thousand times. I have spoken with them as man with man, sometimes with one, sometimes with many in company, and I have seen in them nothing different in form from that of man.

From all my experience, which is now of many years, I can say and affirm that angels are in form entirely men, that they have faces, eyes, ears, body, arms, hands, and feet; that they see one another, hear one another, and talk together; in a word that there is nothing whatever wanting to them that belongs to men, except that they are not clothed over all with a material body. I have seen them in their light, which exceeds the noonday light of the world by many degrees, and in that light all their features were seen more distinctly and clearly than the faces of men are seen on earth. It has been granted me also to see an angel of the inmost heaven. He had a more radiant and resplendent face than the angels of the lower heavens. I observed him attentively, and he had a human form in all perfection.

## HOW ANGELS ARE SEEN BY MEN.

Angels cannot be seen by man with the eyes of the body, but with the eyes of the spirit within him, because this is in the spiritual world and all things of the body in the natural world. And yet man sees these things when he is withdrawn from the sight of the body, and the sight of his spirit is opened, as takes place in a moment when it is the pleasure of the Lord that he should see them. Then man does not know but he sees them. with the eyes of the body. In this way angels were seen by Abraham, Lot, Manoah, and the prophets. In this way, also, the Lord was seen by the disciples after the resurrection. In the same way, too, angels have been seen by me. Because the prophets saw thus, they were called seers and having their eyes open.

## THE LORD'S DIVINE IS IN HUMAN FORM.

All the angels in the heavens perceive the Lord under no other form than the human; and, what is remarkable, those who are in the higher heavens cannot think in any other way of the Divine.

That the men of old time had an idea of the Divine Being as human, is evident from the Divine manifestations to Abraham, Lot, Joshua, Gideon, Manoah and his wife, and others, who, though they saw God as man, still adored Him as the God of the universe, calling Him the God of heaven and earth, and Jehovah.

## THE SUN IN HEAVEN.

Though the sun of the world does not appear in heaven, nor anything from that sun, yet there is a sun there, light and heat and all things as in the world, with innumerable more, but not from the same origin; for the things in heaven are spiritual, and the things in the world are natural. The Sun of heaven is the Lord, the light there is Divine truth, and the heat is Divine good, which proceed from the Lord as a Sun. From this origin are all things that exist and are seen in the heavens.

That the Lord is actually seen in heaven as the Sun, has not only been told me by angels, but has also been given me at times to see.

## LIGHT AND HEAT IN HEAVEN.

That there is light in heaven those cannot apprehend who think only from nature; when yet in the heavens there is light so great that it exceeds by many degrees the noonday light of the world. The brightness and splendor of the light of heaven are such, as cannot be described.

The heat of heaven, like the light of heaven, is everywhere varied, differing in the celestial kingdom from what it is in the spiritual kingdom, and differing in each society — not only in degree but also in quality.

## CHANGES OF STATE OF ANGELS.

Angels are not constantly in the same state as to love, and so they are not in the same state as to wisdom. Sometimes they are in a state of intense love, sometimes in a state of love less intense. The state decreases gradually from its greatest degree to its least. From the last state they return again to the first, and so on. These changes succeed one another with variety.

**The Lord** does not produce their changes of state, since He like the sun is always inflowing with heat and light, that is, with love and wisdom; but the cause is in themselves forasmuch as they love what is their own and this continually leads them away.

## TIME IN HEAVEN.

The angels know nothing of the terms of time, such as year, month, week, day, hour, to-day, to-morrow, yesterday. When they hear them from man in place of them they perceive states and what belong to states.

The same is the case with the four seasons of the year, spring, summer, autumn, and winter; with the four times of day, morning, noon, evening, and night; and with the four ages of man, infancy, youth, manhood, and old age.

Since angels have no notion of time, they have a different idea of eternity from that which men of the earth have. By eternity they perceive infinite state, not infinite time.

## GARMENTS OF ANGELS.

Since angels are men and live together as men with men on earth, they have garments and dwellings and other such things, yet with the difference that they have all things in greater perfection, because they are in a more perfect state.

Their garments correspond to their intelligence, and so all in the heavens are seen clothed according to their intelligence; and because the intelligence of one exceeds that of another, so are the garments of oue superior in excellence to those of another. But angels of the inmost heaven are not clothed.

That the garments of angels really are garments, is evident from this, that they not only see them, but also feel them; and also that they have many garments, and that they put them on and put them off; and those which are not in use they preserve, and when they have use for them put them on again. That they are clothed with various garments, I have seen a thousand times. I inquired whence they had their garments, and they said that it was from the Lord, and that they are sometimes clothed with them unconsciously. They said also that their garments are changed according to their changes of state.

## HABITATIONS OF ANGELS.

Whenever I have spoken with angels face to face, I have been with them in their dwellings. These dwellings are quite like dwellings on earth, which we call houses, but more beautiful. In them are chambers, parlors, and bedrooms, in great number: they have also courts, and are surrounded with gardens, lawns, and shrubberies. Where they live in company together, their houses are contiguous one to another, disposed in the form of a city, with avenues, streets, and public squares, quite like cities on earth.

I have seen palaces of heaven of such magnificence as cannot be described.

There are also angels who do not live in society, but separate, house by house. These dwell in the midst of heaven, because they are the best of angels.

The houses in which angels dwell, are not built as are houses in the world, but are given to them gratuitously by the Lord, to every one according to his reception of good and truth.

## SPACE IN HEAVEN.

All going from place to place in the spiritual world is effected by change of state of the interiors, so that change of place is nothing else than change of state. In this way also I have been conducted by the Lord into the heavens, and likewise to the earths in the universe, and this as to my spirit, while the body remained in the same place.

From the same cause also, in the spiritual world one appears in presence to another, if only he intensely desires his presence: for thus he sees him in thought, and presents himself in his state: and conversely, one is removed from another so far as he is averse to him.

## GOVERNMENTS IN HEAVEN.

Government in the Lord's celestial kingdom is called *Justice*, because all there are in the good of love to the Lord from the Lord. Government there is of the Lord alone: He leads them and teaches them in the affairs of life.

Government in the Lord's spiritual kingdom is called *Judgment;* because they are in spiritual good, which is the good of charity toward the neighbor. These also are led by the Lord, but mediately; and therefore they have governors. They have also laws, according to which they live together.

Such governors do not rule and command, but minister and serve.

## DIVINE WORSHIP IN HEAVEN.

Divine worship in the heavens is not unlike Divine worship on earth as to externals, but as to internals it differs. In the heavens, as on earth, there are doctrines, there are preachings, and there are temples. The doctrines agree as to essentials, but are of more interior wisdom in the higher heavens than in the lower. The preachings are according to the doctrines; and as they have houses and palaces, so likewise they have temples, in which there is preaching.

Divine worship itself, in the heavens, does not however consist in frequenting temples, and in hearing preaching, but in a life of love, charity, and faith, according to doctrines; preachings in temples serve only as means of instruction in matters of life.

The sacred edifices in the latter kingdom are not called temples, but houses of God; and here they are without magnificence; but in the spiritual kingdom they are magnificent in various degree.

All the preachers are from the Lord's spiritual kingdom, and none from the celestial kingdom.

## POWER OF ANGELS.

The power of angels is so great, that if I should bring forward all that I have seen in regard to it, it would exceed belief. If anything there resists, which is to be removed because contrary to Divine order, they cast it down and overturn it merely by an effort of the will and a look. Numbers are of no avail against them, nor arts, cunning, and leagues, for they see all, and disperse them in a moment.

It is to be known, however, that angels have no power at all from themselves, but that all their power is from the Lord; and that they are only so far powers as they acknowledge this. Whoever of them believes that he has power from himself, becomes instantly so weak that he cannot even resist one evil spirit.

## SPEECH OF ANGELS.

Angelic speech, just like human speech, is distinguished into words, and is also uttered by sound and heard by sound; for angels like men have mouth, tongue, and ears, and also an atmosphere, in which the sound of their speech is articulated.

All in the whole heaven have one language, and they all understand one another, from whatever society they are, whether near or distant. Language is not learned there, but is natural to every one. I have been told that the first language of men on our earth was in agreement with angelic language, because they had it from heaven;

and that the Hebrew language agrees with it in some things.

Because the speech of angels proceeds immediately from their affection, angels can express in a minute what man cannot express in half an hour; and they can also by a few words present what has been written on many pages.

## SPEECH OF ANGELS WITH MAN.

Angels who speak with man do not speak in their own language, but in the man's language, and also in other languages with which the man is acquainted, but not in languages unknown to the man.

The speech of an angel or spirit with man is heard as sonorously as the speech of man with man, yet not by others who stand near, but by himself alone. The reason is, that the speech of an angel or spirit flows first into man's thought, and by an inner way into his organ of hearing, thus affecting it from within; but the speech of man with man flows first into the air, and by an outward way into his organ of hearing, thus affecting it from without.

To speak with spirits, however, is at this day seldom given, since it is dangerous; for then the spirits know that they are with man, which otherwise they do not know; and evil spirits are such that they hold man in deadly hatred and desire nothing more than to destroy him, both soul and body.

They who speak with angels of heaven, see at the same time things that are in heaven, because they see from the light of heaven, in which their interiors are, and the angels also see through them things that are on the earth.

I have been informed how the Lord spoke with the prophets through whom the Word was given. He did not speak with them as with the ancients, by an influx into their interiors, but through spirits who were sent to them, and thus inspired with words which they dictated to the prophets.

## WRITINGS IN HEAVEN.

That there are writings, in heaven, has been provided by the Lord for the sake of the Word. Angels also have the Word, and they read it equally as men on earth; from it also are their doctrinals, and from it they preach. The writing in the inmost heaven consists of various inflected and circumflected forms, and the inflections and circumflexions are according to the form of heaven; by them angels express the arcana of their wisdom, and also many things which they cannot utter by words; and what is wonderful, angels know that writing without training or a teacher, it being implanted in them like their speech itself. I have been told that the most ancient people on this earth also, before letters were invented, had such writing; and that it was translated into the letters of the Hebrew language — which letters in ancient times were all inflected, and not any of them, as at this day, terminated as lines.

In the lower heavens there are not such writings, but writings similar to what we have in the world, in similar letters — yet not intelligible to man, because they are in angelic language, and angelic language is such that it has nothing in common with human languages. This writing too, which I have also seen, involves in a few words more than a man can describe by pages. They have the Word written in this way in the lower heavens, and by heavenly forms in the inmost heaven.

## WISDOM OF THE ANGELS.

Angels can express by one word what a man cannot express by a thousand words; and moreover in one angelic word there are innumerable things which cannot be expressed by the words of human language. Interior angels also can know the whole

25

life of one speaking, from the sound and a few words; for they perceive from this sound, variegated by ideas in words, his ruling love, on which everything of his life is as it were inscribed. Their wisdom, in comparison with human wisdom, is as a myriad to one. The wisdom of angels of the third or inmost heaven is incomprehensible, even to those who are in the lowest heaven.

## INNOCENCE OF ANGELS IN, HEAVEN.

Innocence is the *esse* of all good, and hence good is so far good as innocence is in it, consequently wisdom is so far wisdom as it partakes of innocence — and that hence no one can enter heaven unless he has innocence.

## CONJUNCTION OF HEAVEN WITH MAN BY THE WORD.

I have been informed from heaven that the most ancient people had immediate revelation, and there was at that time conjunction of the Lord with the human race. After their time there was mediate revelation by correspondences. After the knowledge of correspondences and representations was forgotten, the Word was written, in which all the words and their meanings are correspondences, and thus contain a spiritual or internal sense, in which angels are. For this reason, when man reads the Word and perceives it according to the sense of the letter, or the outward sense, the angels perceive it according to the inner or spiritual sense. Hence it is that after man removed himself from heaven and broke the bond, there was provided by the Lord a means of conjunction of heaven with man through the Word.

The man of this earth is such that he cannot receive immediate revelation and be instructed by that means in Divine truths, like the inhabitants of other earths. For the man of this earth is more in worldly things than the men of other earths.

## HEAVEN AND HELL ARE FROM THE HUMAN RACE.

In the whole heaven there is not one angel who was so created from the beginning, nor in hell any devil who was created an angel of light and cast down; but all, both in heaven and in hell, are from the human race. Hell taken as a whole is what is called the devil and satan.

It has been given me to speak with all with whom I have ever been acquainted in the life of the body, after their decease: with some for days, with some for months, and with some for a year; and also with others, so many that I should say too few if I should say a hundred thousand; many of whom were in heaven, and many in hell. I have also spoken with some two days after their decease and have told them that funeral services were now being held and preparations made for their interment. To which they said that it was well to reject that which had served them for a body and its functions in the world; and they wished me to say that they were not dead but that they live and are men now as before, and that they had only migrated from one world into the other, and that they are not aware of having lost anything, since they are in a body with its senses as before and also in understanding and in will as before, and that they have thoughts and affections, sensations and desires, similar to those which they had in the world.

## THE HEATHEN IN HEAVEN.

That gentiles are saved as well as Christians, may be known by those who know what it is that makes heaven with man; for heaven is in man, and those who have heaven in themselves come into heaven. Heaven in man is to acknowledge the Divine and to be led by the Divine. The first and primary thing of every religion is to acknowledge the Divine. It is known that gentiles live a moral life as well as Christians, and many of them a better life than Christians.

I have learned in many ways that gentiles who have led a moral life, in obedience and subordination, and have lived in mutual charity according to their religion, and have thus received something of conscience, are accepted in the other life and are there instructed with solicitous care by angels; and that when they are being instructed. they behave themselves modestly, intelligently, and wisely, and easily receive truths and adopt them.

There are in the universe many earths and all full of inhabitants, of whom scarcely any know that the Lord has assumed the Human in our earth. Yet because they adore the Divine under a human form, they are accepted and led of the Lord. Among gentiles in heaven the Africans are most beloved, for they receive the goods and truths of heaven more easily than others.

## LITTLE CHILDREN IN HEAVEN.

Every child wheresoever he is born, whether within the Church or out of it, whether of pious parents or of impious, when he dies is received by the Lord and is educated in heaven: and afterward, as he is perfected in intelligence and wisdom, he is introduced into heaven and becomes an angel.

Little children as soon as they are raised up, which takes place immediately after death, are taken into heaven and delivered to angel women who in the life of the body tenderly loved children and at the same time loved God. These. because in the world they loved all children from a motherly tenderness. receive them as their own. and the little children also love them instinctively as their own mothers. There are as many children with each one as she desires from a spiritual parental affection It is to be known that children in heaven do not advance in age beyond early manhood and remain in this to eternity. No one of the other life ever suffers punishment on account of hereditary evil, because it is not his, thus it is not his fault that he is such.

## RICH AND POOR IN HEAVEN.

A man may acquire riches and accumulate wealth so far as opportunity is given, provided it be not done with craft and fraud: that he may eat and drink delicately, provided he does not place his life therein: that he may dwell in magnificence according to his condition, may converse with others in their manner, frequent places of amusement, talk about the affairs of the world; and that he has no need to walk as a devotee with a sad and sorrowful face and drooping head, but may be joyful and cheerful; nor need he give his goods to the poor, except so far as affection leads him. In a word he may live outwardly quite like a man of the world; and these things do not hinder a man's coming into heaven, provided that inwardly in himself he thinks properly about God, and acts sincerely and justly with his neighbor.

I have spoken with some after death who while they lived in the world, renounced the world and gave themselves up to a life almost solitary, in order that by an abstraction of the thoughts from worldly things, they might be at leisure for pious meditations, believing that they should thus enter the way of heaven. But these in the other life are of a sad disposition: they despise others who are not like themselves, they are indignant that they do not attain greater happiness than others, believing that they have merited it, they do not care for others, and turn away from offices of charity. A life of charity towards the neighbor, which is to do what is just and right in every work and in every function, leads to heaven, but not a life of piety without charity.

The poor come into heaven not on account of their poverty, but on account of their life. The life of every one follows him, whether he be rich or poor. There is no peculiar mercy for one more than for the other; he is received who has lived well, and he is rejected who has lived ill. Moreover poverty seduces and draws man away from heaven as well as wealth.

## MARRIAGES IN HEAVEN.

Since heaven is of the human race and angels are therefore of both sexes, and since from creation woman is for man and man for woman, thus the one is the other's, and since this love is innate in both, it follows that there are marriages in heaven as well as on earth.

Marriage in heaven is the conjunction of two into one mind. The mind consists of two parts, the one of which is called the understanding and the other the will. When these two parts make one, then they are called one mind. The husband then makes the part which is called the understanding and the wife that which is called the will. When this conjunction comes lower down into what is of their body it is then perceived and felt as love, and this love is marriage love.

Marriages in heaven differ from marriages upon earth in this, that marriages on earth are also for the procreation of offspring, but not in heaven; instead of that procreation, there is in heaven a procreation of good and truth.

Marriages on earth, because they are the seminaries of the human race and also of the angels of heaven, are therefore most holy in the sight of the angels of heaven.

## FUNCTIONS OF ANGELS.

In the heavens, as on earth, there are many administrations, for there are ecclesiastical affairs, there are civil affairs, and there are domestic affairs.

All the societies in the heavens are distinct according to uses. There are some societies whose functions are to take care of infants; others to instruct and educate them as they grow up. There are some societies that teach the simple good from the Christian world, and others that teach and lead the various gentile nations. There are some societies that defend those who have come recently from the world, from infestations by evil spirits; some that are near those who are in the lower earth; and also some that are near those who are near those who are in the hells. There are some also that are with those who are raised from the dead.

## HEAVENLY JOY AND HAPPINESS.

Those who are in heaven are continually advancing to the spring of life, and the more thousands of years they live, to a spring so much the more joyful and happy, and this to eternity, with increase according to the progressions and degrees of their love, charity, and faith. Women who have died old and worn out with age, if they have lived in faith in the Lord, in charity to the neighbor, and in happy marriage love with a husband, with the succession of years come more and more into the flower of youth and early womanhood, and into beauty which exceeds all idea of beauty ever perceivable by our sight and amazes those who behold it.

## IMMENSITY OF HEAVEN.

How immense the heaven of the Lord is, may also be evident from this, that all the planets visible to the eye in our solar system are earths, and moreover that there are innumerable ones in the universe, and all full of inhabitants.

## THE LORD RULES THE HELLS.

The Lord is the God of heaven, and all the government of the heavens is in the hands of the Lord; and since the relation of heaven to hell, and of hell to heaven, is as that between two opposites, which act contrary to each other, it is necessary that He who rules the one should also rule the other.

Hitherto it has been believed in the world that there is one devil who presides over the hells; and that he was created an angel of light, but after he became rebellious, was cast down with his crew into hell. That this belief has prevailed, is because in the Word mention is made of the devil and Satan when yet by the devil and Satan is meant hell.

## THE LORD CASTS NO ONE INTO HELL, BUT THE SPIRIT CASTS HIMSELF.

An opinion has prevailed that God turns away His face from man, and casts him into hell, and that He is angry with him on account of evil; and further, that God punishes man and does evil to him. The genuine doctrine of the church, which is from the spiritual sense of the Word, teaches otherwise, namely that God never turns away His face from man and that He does not cast any one into hell, and that He is not angry with any one.

WS - #0214 - 040923 - C0 - 229/152/2 - PB - 9780259593157 - Gloss Lamination